THE STORY OF THE STAR-SPANGLED BANNER

By the Dawn's Early Light

THE STORY OF THE STAR-SPANGLED BANNER

By the Dawn's Early Light

BY

STEVEN KROLL

ILLUSTRATED BY

DAN ANDREASEN

SCHOLASTIC
HARDCOVER

SCHOLASTIC INC.

New York

Grateful acknowledgment is made for permission to reproduce the original manuscript
of "The Star-Spangled Banner" and the engraving of Francis Scott Key
from the collection of The Maryland Historical Society, Baltimore, Maryland;
for the map of Washington in 1814 from the Thomas G. Machen collection
of the Historical Society of Washington, D.C.; to Scott Sheads at Fort McHenry
for fact checking the manuscript; and to Randa Kirschbaum for setting the music
for "The Star-Spangled Banner."

Library of Congress Cataloging-in-Publication Data

Kroll, Steven.
By the dawn's early light : the story of the Star-spangled banner
/ by Steven Kroll : illustrated by Dan Andreasen.
p. cm.
Includes bibliographical references (p. 39).
Summary: An account of the writing of the "Star-Spangled Banner,"
detailing how Key was actually behind enemy lines at the time
seeking release of a captured friend from the British, who would not
allow their departure until the bombardment of Baltimore was completed.
ISBN 0-590-45054-9
1. Star-spangled banner (song)—Juvenile literature. 2. Key,
Francis Scott, 1779–1843—Juvenile literature. 3. Poets,
American—19th century—Biography—Juvenile literature. 4. United
States—History—War of 1812—Juvenile literature. 5. Lawyers—
United States—Biography—Juvenile literature. [1. Star-spangled
banner (Song) 2. Key, Francis Scott, 1779–1843. 3. Poets,
American. 4. Lawyers.] I. Andreasen, Dan, ill. II. Title.
PS2167.S73K76 1993
349.73′092—dc20
[B]   92-27101
CIP
AC

12 11 10 9 8 7 6 5 4 3 2 1   3 4 5 6 7 8/9

Printed in the U.S.A.   37

First Scholastic printing, February 1994

The illustrations in this book were done in oil paint.
Book design by David Turner

To the free and the brave
S.K.

For Sharon, my best friend
D.A.

The War of 1812

Between 1793 and 1814, France, led by the power-hungry Napoleon, waged war against many European countries.

As England began needing more sailors for the Royal Navy, there were fewer and fewer British commercial ships. Soon the United States had pretty much taken over trade between the French and Spanish colonies and Europe.

England and France tried to impose restrictions on American shipping, and the Royal Navy began boarding American ships and seizing both British deserters and American sailors for their service. Finally, on June 18, 1812, a poorly prepared United States declared war on Great Britain.

For almost two years there were battles on land and sea. Then, in March 1814, Napoleon was defeated in Europe, and Britain turned full attention to America.

On August 18th of that year, British forces reached the mouth of the Patuxent River. Between the 19th and the 25th, British troops defeated the inexperienced American militia at Bladensburg, Maryland, burned a defenseless Washington, and returned to their ships.

The burning of the Executive Mansion (now called the White House) by the British in the War of 1812.

August 31, 1814

Francis Scott Key was a well-known Washington lawyer. He lived just outside the city center in Georgetown where he was also a lieutenant in the Georgetown Light Artillery. Since the burning of Washington on August 24th, he had been on duty every day.

On August 31st, he had only just come home, when there was a sharp knock at his door.

He flung it open, and there was Richard West, his brother-in-law.

"The British have arrested Dr. Beanes!" said Richard. "He's a prisoner on one of their ships."

Francis was outraged. Dr. William Beanes was a close friend from Upper Marlborough, Maryland. "But why?" he almost shouted.

"Dr. Beanes was looking after wounded British soldiers. After the army left, three stragglers began making trouble. The doctor had them thrown in jail. The British got angry—"

"Something must be done!" said Francis.

"A few of us hoped you might use your influence with President Madison."

Francis got released from military duty. Early the next morning, after a hug from his wife, Polly, and their six children, he mounted his horse and rode into Washington.

The smell of burning was everywhere. The Capitol was gone, along with the Executive Mansion. Temporary presidential quarters had been set up at the French Minister's house, and when Francis walked inside, everyone looked worried.

He was shown into a front room with a guard at the door. The president sat alone. He was pale and hollow-eyed and looked very small.

Francis made his request. Mr. Madison turned and smiled sadly. "I give you permission to visit the British fleet as an official American envoy under a flag of truce. John Mason, Commissary General of Prisoners, will allow Colonel John S. Skinner, his agent in charge of prisoner exchange, to go with you."

"Thank you, sir," said Francis.

He returned home and asked Polly to take the children to Terra Rubra, their estate in western Maryland. The following day, he set off through stifling heat for Baltimore.

General Samuel Smith was busy preparing his men for the defense of Baltimore and Fort McHenry when Francis arrived. Colonel Skinner was there and listened carefully to President Madison's instructions. He mentioned that he knew Dr. Beanes personally and had in his possession letters from wounded British officers describing the doctor's kindness to them after the Battle of Bladensburg. He arranged to hire a small boat so he and Francis could sail down Chesapeake Bay to meet the British.

By the time Francis and Colonel Skinner were ready to leave, the heat was breaking and a storm was coming up. When it began to pour, they took shelter at a local inn. The rain continued, and it wasn't until September 5th that they were able to sail their small cartel boat with its white flag of truce down the Patapsco River toward Chesapeake Bay.

They searched for the British fleet until nightfall, but they had no luck until late in the afternoon of September 7th. The tall ships were lying off the mouth of the Potomac. Colonel Skinner sighted Vice Admiral Sir Alexander Cochrane's eighty-gun flagship, H.M.S. *Tonnant*. As they drew closer, Francis could see the line of gun ports, black checkerboard squares against a yellow background.

They reached the *Tonnant*. Francis and the colonel climbed aboard and were taken to Admiral Cochrane's cabin.

The admiral was friendly but formal. "No," he said when Francis finished his plea. "As a noncombatant, Dr. Beanes had no right to arrest those men."

Francis explained that the doctor might not have realized what he was doing, that he could not have violated his neutrality because by then the British were no longer occupying the territory.

The admiral gestured to a midshipman. "Call in General Ross and Admiral Cockburn."

They arrived almost at once. Major General Sir Robert Ross was tall and imposing, Rear Admiral Sir George Cockburn, red-faced and grim.

Once more Francis presented his arguments and his official letters. This time he stressed the letters of praise for Dr. Beanes from the wounded British officers.

"A pack of nonsense," said Admiral Cockburn. "We must take Beanes to Halifax and see that he's punished there."

"I do not agree," said General Ross. "I am moved by these letters from wounded officers, and as co-commander of our expeditionary forces, I will release the prisoner. However, all three of these men will remain with us until after we have completed our attack on Baltimore."

Francis and the colonel shared a look of alarm. Then they were hurried out to a small hold in the ship's prow. Dr. Beanes was there and greeted them warmly. When his two friends told him what was happening, he was horrified.

"And we must sit and watch while our country is attacked?" he exclaimed.

"I'm afraid so," Colonel Skinner replied.

The three Americans were put up on the frigate *Surprise,* and for three days the British fleet crept up Chesapeake Bay.

Meanwhile, Baltimore was getting ready. Though inexperienced, the militia was on call. The city was ringed by trenches and ramparts built by citizens. At star-shaped Fort McHenry, out on Whetstone Point overlooking the Patapsco River, a thousand troops were under the command of Major George Armistead. They had thrown up barriers outside the moat, placed sandbags around the powder magazine, and sunk many small ships and barges in the north channel of the river to slow enemy progress. They had also stationed a half-dozen small gunboats between the sunken hulls and the city.

There was a bold, new flag flying over the fort. Forty-two by thirty feet, fifteen stars and fifteen stripes, it was the work of Mary Pickersgill and her daughter, Caroline.

On Saturday, September 10th, the British fleet anchored off North Point at the mouth of the Patapsco River. Francis, Colonel Skinner, and Dr. Beanes were hustled from the *Surprise* back to their own small boat. Admiral Cochrane had decided to take personal command of the bombardment. He wanted the smaller, faster frigate as his flagship.

Sunday morning, Baltimore's church bells called the militia to arms. Monday, boats filled with British soldiers in scarlet uniforms began leaving for shore. Francis watched grimly. Things did not look good for the Americans.

With the troops underway on land, the fleet began moving upriver. As the ships came within view of Fort McHenry, the Stars and Stripes were waving overhead.

Later that afternoon, word came from shore. The Americans had retreated to positions outside the city. General Ross had been killed.

A silence seemed to fall over the fleet, but preparations continued. Francis, Dr. Beanes, and Colonel Skinner spent a restless night as sixteen smaller British ships moved into the shallower water closer to the fort.

At dawn the bombardment began. The noise was so great and the smell of burning powder so strong that the three hostages were forced to take refuge in their cabin. When the response from the fort seemed to die away for a moment, it became clear that the Americans' thirty-six-pound shells were not reaching the ships. But then the heavy shelling and rocketing began again and went on hour after hour.

At dusk Francis crawled out onto the deck. "Can you see the flag?" Dr. Beanes called after him.

Francis squinted through the smoke and the din and the glow of the setting sun. "The flag is flying," he replied.

Soon after, it began to rain. Thunder and lightning joined the booming of the guns. Very late that night, Francis struggled out on deck again. Though he could not know it, at that moment the British were trying to land a thousand men at Ferry Branch. An American sentry discovered them and Fort McHenry began to fire. As the barges fled, every available American gun pursued them.

The rainy night sky was suddenly lit up, and in that moment Francis could see the flag again. It was soaked now and drooping from its staff, but it was there, still there.

By dawn the rain had stopped and the fight was over. Peering through the clouds, Francis, Dr. Beanes, and Colonel Skinner strained to see what flag was flying over the fort. Had the British triumphed in the night? But no, there it was, unfurling in the breeze, the Stars and Stripes!

All his life, Francis had written poetry. He reached into his pocket and found an old letter. With the tune to the song, "To Anacreon in Heaven" in mind, he scribbled *O say can you see* and then *by the dawn's early light.*

He wrote a few more lines, crossed out a few, but there wasn't much time. Already redcoats were leaving for the ships. The fleet was abandoning the assault!

The sails of the little cartel boat were returned to the members of its American crew. By afternoon, Francis, Dr. Beanes, and Colonel Skinner were back in Baltimore.

Cheering crowds were everywhere. The three men went straight to the Indian Queen Hotel on Baltimore Street, rested and had supper, but later that night, Francis finished the four stanzas of his poem.

The next day he went to visit his brother-in-law, Judge Joseph Nicholson, who had been at Fort McHenry. Judge Nicholson loved the new poem. "Let's get it printed," he insisted.

The judge rushed over to the *Baltimore American*, but the printers weren't back from defending the fort. A young apprentice, Samuel Sands, agreed to set the verses in type and run off the handbills. Because Francis hadn't thought of a title, Judge Nicholson came up with "The Defense of Fort McHenry," but it wasn't long before everyone was singing what had come to be known as "The Star-Spangled Banner."

AUTHOR'S NOTE

For those concerned with additional detail, it was the fort's storm flag, measuring twenty-five by seventeen feet, that was flying overhead during the battle. The larger flag, the fort's garrison flag, was raised in celebration as Francis Scott Key sailed back to Baltimore. Both flags had been made by Mary Pickersgill.

After writing his poem, Key returned to Terra Rubra and then to Georgetown and his successful law practice. When his friend Andrew Jackson became president in 1829, he was appointed United States District Attorney for the District of Columbia. Always opposed to slavery, he was a founder of the American Colonization Society, which began a settlement of freed slaves on the west coast of Africa called Liberia. He and Polly had eleven children altogether and eventually retired to Terra Rubra.

With the collapse of the assault on Baltimore, the British fleet sailed to Jamaica. A peace treaty was signed at Ghent (in what is now Belgium) on December 24, 1814, but word of that did not reach America for some time and the final battle of the war was actually fought and won by Andrew Jackson at New Orleans on January 8, 1815.

Over the years, "The Star-Spangled Banner" became more and more popular. In the 1890s, it became the official song of the Army and the Navy. In 1916, President Woodrow Wilson ordered that it be played on official occasions, but not until 1931 did the Congress, by decree, make the song the national anthem of the United States of America.

O say can you see, ~~through~~ by the dawn's early light,
What so proudly we hail'd at the twilight's last gleaming,
Whose broad stripes & bright stars through the perilous fight
O'er the ramparts we watch'd, were so gallantly streaming?
  And the rocket's red glare, the bomb bursting in air,
  Gave proof through the night that our flag was still there,
O say does that star spangled banner yet wave
O'er the land of the free & the home of the brave?

On the shore dimly seen through the mists of the deep,
Where the foe's haughty host in dread silence reposes,
What is that which the breeze, o'er the towering steep,
As it fitfully blows, half conceals, half discloses?
  Now it catches the gleam of the morning's first beam,
  In full glory reflected now shines in the stream,
'Tis the star-spangled banner — O long may it wave
O'er the land of the free & the home of the brave!

And where is that band who so vauntingly swore,
That the havoc of war & the battle's confusion
A home & a Country should leave us no more?
— ~~Their~~
  Their blood has wash'd out their foul footstep's pollution.
  No refuge could save the hireling & slave
From the terror of flight or the gloom of the grave,
And the star-spangled banner in triumph doth wave
O'er the land of the free & the home of the brave.

O thus be it ever when freemen shall stand
Between their lov'd home & the war's desolation!
Blest with vict'ry & peace may the heav'n rescued land
Praise the power that hath made & preserv'd us a nation!
  Then conquer we must, when our cause it is just,
  And this be our motto — "In God is our trust,"
And the star-spangled banner in triumph shall wave
O'er the land of the free & the home of the brave. —

This is a photograph of the original manuscript of the poem that Francis Scott Key wrote in his room at the Indian Queen Hotel on Baltimore Street the evening after he had witnessed the Battle of Baltimore.

The Star-Spangled Banner

Words by
Francis Scott Key
(1779-1843)

Music by
J. Stafford Smith
(1750-1836)

2.

On the shore dimly seen through the mists of the deep,
Where the foe's haughty host in the dread silence reposes,
What is that which the breeze, o'er the towering steep,
As it fitfully blows, half conceals, half discloses?
Now it catches the gleam of the morning's first beam,
In full glory reflected now shines in the stream.
'Tis the star-spangled banner, oh, long may it wave
O'er the land of the free and the home of the brave!

3.

And where is that band who so vauntingly swore
That the havoc of war and the battle's confusion
A home and a country should leave us no more?
Their blood has wash'd out their foul footstep's pollution.
No refuge could save the hireling and slave
From the terror of flight or the gloom of the grave,
And the star-spangled banner in triumph doth wave
O'er the land of the free and the home of the brave.

4.

Oh, thus be it ever when freemen shall stand
Between their lov'd home and the war's desolation!
Blest with vict'ry and peace may the heav'n-rescued land
Praise the power that hath made and preserv'd us a nation!
Then conquer we must, when our cause it is just,
And this be our motto, "In God is our Trust,"
And the star-spangled banner in triumph shall wave
O'er the land of the free and the home of the brave.

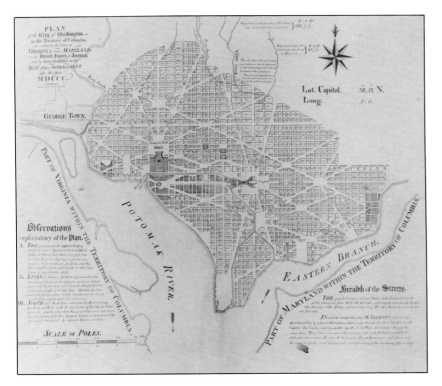

Map of Washington D.C. in 1814.

Etching of Francis Scott Key.
(*Artist unknown.*)

THE BATTLE OF BALTIMORE, September 12–14, 1814

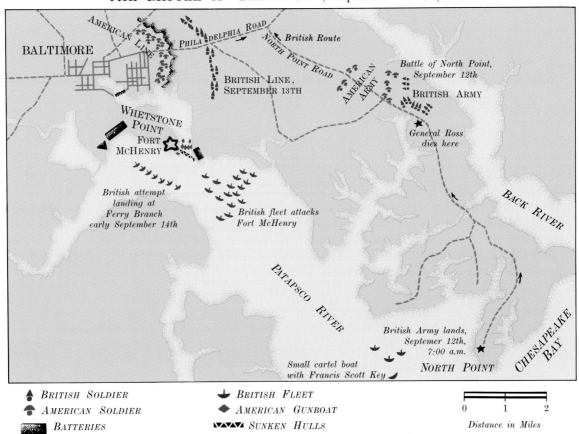

Map of the Battle of Baltimore with significant landmarks and important events leading up to the battle.

BIBLIOGRAPHY

Bates, Helen Dixon, *Francis Scott Key*. New York: Whittlesey House, McGraw-Hill Book Company, 1936.

Carmer, Carl, *A Flag for the Fort*. New York: Julian Messner, Inc., 1952.

Fradin, Dennis B., *The Flag of the United States*. Chicago: Children's Press, 1988.

Georgiady, Nicholas Peter, *Our National Anthem*. Chicago: Follett Publishing Company, 1963.

Holland, Rupert Sargent, *Freedom's Flag: The Story of Francis Scott Key*. Philadelphia: Macrae-Smith Company, 1943.

Parrish, Thomas, *The American Flag*. New York: Simon and Schuster, Inc., 1973.

Patterson, Lillie, *Francis Scott Key, Poet and Patriot*. Illustrated by Vic Dowd. Champaign, Illinois: Garrard Publishing Company, 1963.

Sheads, Scott, *The Rockets' Red Glare: The Maritime Defense of Baltimore in 1814*. Centreville, Maryland: Tidewater Publishers, 1986.

Spier, Peter, *The Star-Spangled Banner*. Garden City, New York: Doubleday, 1973.

Stevenson, Augusta, *Francis Scott Key, Maryland Boy*. Indianapolis: Bobbs-Merrill Company, 1960.

Weybright, Victor, *Spangled Banner: The Story of Francis Scott Key*. New York: Farrar, Rinehart, Inc., 1935.

Williams, Earl P., Jr., *What You Should Know About the American Flag*. Gettysburg, Pennsylvania: Thomas Publications, 1987.

INDEX